A Benjamin Blog
and His Inquisitive Dog
Guide

India

Anita Ganeri

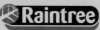
Raintree

Raintree is an imprint of Capstone Global Library Limited, a company incorporated in England and Wales having its registered office at 7 Pilgrim Street, London, EC4V 6LB – Registered company number: 6695582

www.raintreepublishers.co.uk
myorders@raintreepublishers.co.uk

Edited by Dan Nunn, Helen Cox Cannons, and Gina Kammer
Designed by Jo Hinton-Malivoire
Picture research by Ruth Blair and Hannah Taylor
Production by Helen McCreath
Originated by Capstone Global Library Ltd
Printed and bound in Dubai by Oriental Press

ISBN 978 1 406 28105 7
18 17 16 15 14
10 9 8 7 6 5 4 3 2 1

British Library Cataloguing in Publication Data
A full catalogue record for this book is available from the British Library.

Acknowledgements
We would like to thank the following for permission to reproduce photographs:

Alamy: brianindia, 17, Paul Prescott, 15, Stephen Ford, 14, Stuart Forster, 24, szefei wong, 12, Thomas Cockrem, 22, travelib history, 7, Universal Images Group Ltd., 11; Corbis: ZUMA Press/Prasanta Biswas, 27; Getty Images: Amar Grover, 18, Ben Edwards, 13, Danita Delimont, 10, DreamPictures, 23, Joao Figueiredo, 6, Kurt Werby, 4, Martin Child, 16, Martin Harvey, 8, Subir Basak, 19; Shutterstock: Globe Turner, 28, Mazzzur, cover, Rajesh Narayanan, 25, saiko3p, 26, 29; Superstock: Steve Vidler, 20, Stock Connection, 9, 21

Every effort has been made to contact copyright holders of material reproduced in this book. Any omissions will be rectified in subsequent printings if notice is given to the publisher.

All the internet addresses (URLs) given in this book were valid at the time of going to press. However, due to the dynamic nature of the internet, some addresses may have changed, or sites may have changed or ceased to exist since publication. While the author and publisher regret any inconvenience this may cause readers, no responsibility for any such changes can be accepted by either the author or the publisher.

Some words are shown in bold, **like this**. You can find out what they mean by looking in the glossary.

Contents

Welcome to India!

Hello! My name is Benjamin Blog and this is Barko Polo, my **inquisitive** dog. (He is named after ancient ace explorer, **Marco Polo**.) We have just got back from our latest adventure – exploring India. We put this book together from some of the blog posts we wrote on the way.

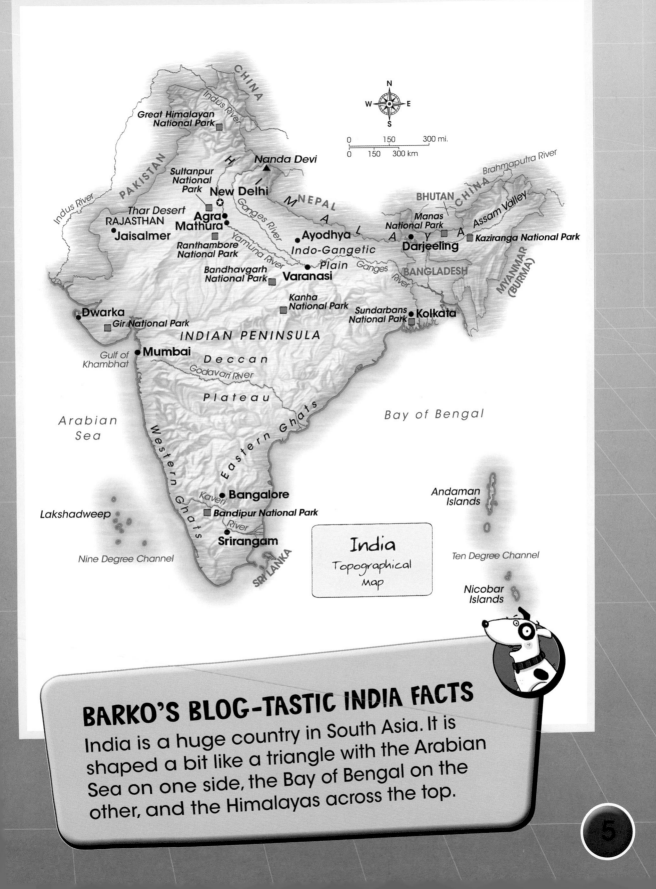

India
Topographical Map

BARKO'S BLOG-TASTIC INDIA FACTS

India is a huge country in South Asia. It is shaped a bit like a triangle with the Arabian Sea on one side, the Bay of Bengal on the other, and the Himalayas across the top.

Historic places

Posted by: Ben Blog | 4 December at 10.00 a.m.

We started our tour at Fatehpur Sikri, the ancient capital city built by the **Mughal emperor** Akbar. He ruled India about 450 years ago. Nobody lives here now, but you can wander around the beautiful palaces and have your picture taken next to the grave of Akbar's favourite elephant.

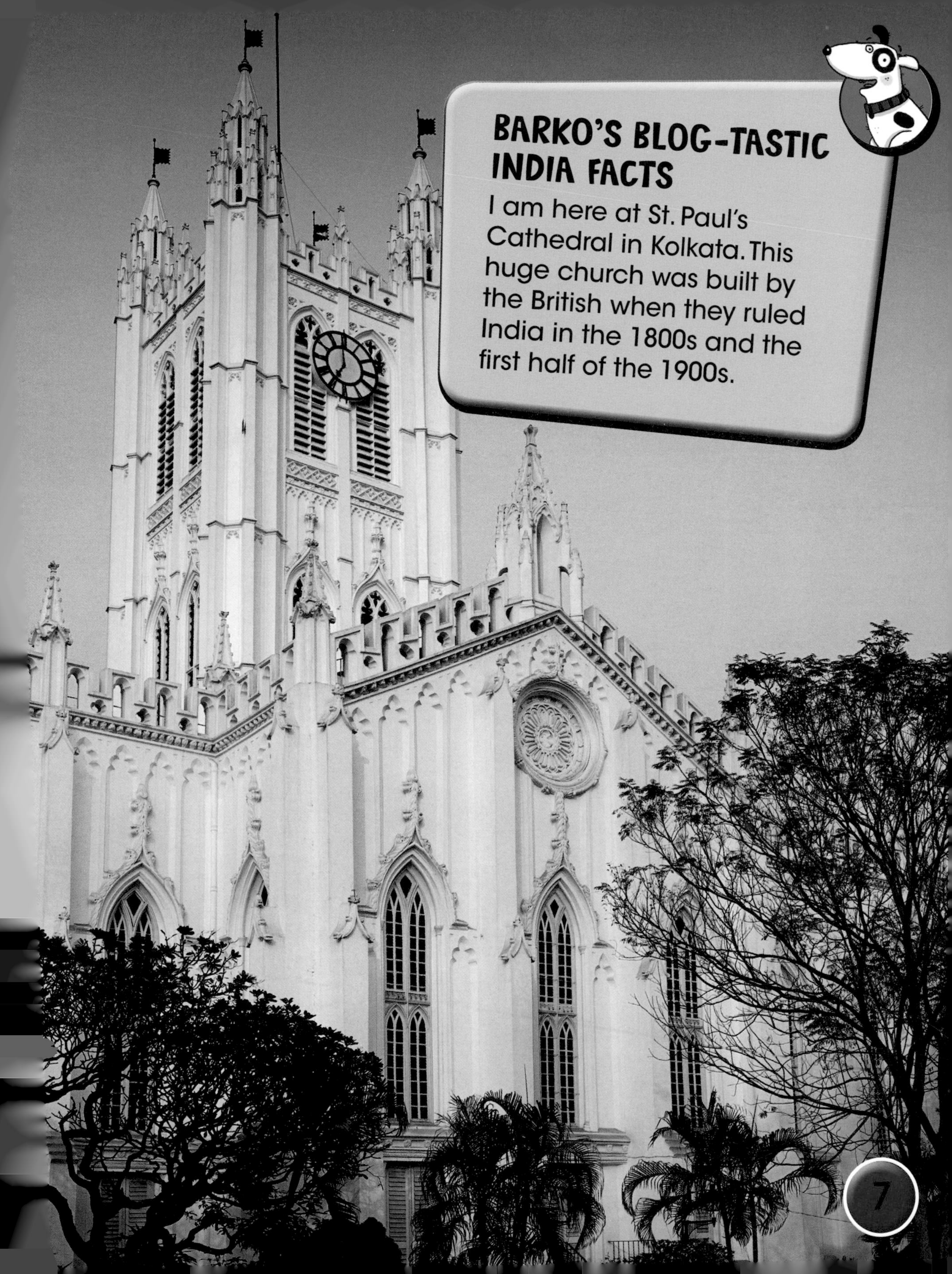

BARKO'S BLOG-TASTIC INDIA FACTS

I am here at St. Paul's Cathedral in Kolkata. This huge church was built by the British when they ruled India in the 1800s and the first half of the 1900s.

Rivers, mountains, and deserts

Posted by: Ben Blog | 18 December at 2.10 p.m.

From Fatehpur Sikri, we caught the train to Varanasi on the banks of the river Ganges. The river flows from the Himalayas, across India, and into the Bay of Bengal. For **Hindus**, it is a holy river. They believe that bathing in the water will wash away any bad things they have done.

BARKO'S BLOG-TASTIC INDIA FACTS

This is Nanda Devi, the second-highest mountain in India. The highest mountain is Kanchenjunga. Nanda Devi is 7,816 metres (25,643 feet) high and part of the awesome Himalayas, the world's highest peaks.

Our next stop was the dusty Thar Desert, where we arrived just in time for the camel festival. It lasts for five days, and people come from all over the desert to buy and sell their camels. There is even a "best-dressed camel" contest. Here is a photo I took of this year's winner.

BARKO'S BLOG-TASTIC INDIA FACTS

In summer, it pours with rain in India. This is called the **monsoon**. Farmers rely on the rain to water their fields, but it can also cause terrible floods.

Crowded cities

Posted by: Ben Blog | 30 March at 4.36 p.m.

This morning we arrived in New Delhi, India's capital city. What a busy, bustling place. We hitched a ride on a **rickshaw** to the Red Fort in the old part of the city. Like Fatehpur Sikri, the Red Fort was built by the **Mughals**, and it gets its name from its massive red **sandstone** walls.

BARKO'S BLOG-TASTIC INDIA FACTS

Many poor Indian people move to cities in search of work and a better life. Some live in overcrowded parts of the city, called **slums**. Some sleep, wash, and cook on the street.

Namaste!

Posted by: Ben Blog | 3 June at 11.55 a.m.

Namaste means "hello" in Hindi. When you say *namaste*, you put your hands together and bow your head. Hindi is the most commonly spoken language in India, especially here in the north. But there are 21 other main languages and many local **dialects** to learn.

BARKO'S BLOG-TASTIC INDIA FACTS

Indian children often live with their parents, aunts, uncles, cousins, and grandparents. The woman on the left is wearing a **sari**. This is usually made from long pieces of cotton or silk.

In the big cities, many people live in large blocks of apartments. But, a short bus ride out of the city, and we are in the countryside. Most Indian people live in small villages and work by farming the land. They live in small, simple houses with their animals outside.

16

BARKO'S BLOG-TASTIC INDIA FACTS

In India, children start school when they are 6 years old. These children are on their way to their modern, city school. In villages, lessons are sometimes held outside with children sitting on the ground.

We have travelled south to Tamil Nadu. It is famous for its temples, such as this one at Srirangam. Most Indians are **Hindus**, who follow the religion of **Hinduism**. A temple is a place where they worship. This stunning tower is the gateway to the temple and is covered in carvings of the Hindu gods and goddesses.

18

BARKO'S BLOG-TASTIC INDIA FACTS

I am celebrating Diwali, the Hindu festival of lights. People light small lamps to guide the god Lord Rama home. Later, there is a spectacular fireworks display.

Feeling hungry?

Posted by: Ben Blog | 3 November at 6.10 p.m.

All this travelling makes Barko and me hungry, so we stopped for an Indian meal. Most Hindus are vegetarians and do not eat meat. They like to eat spicy vegetables with rice or flatbreads. Here in the south, crispy rice pancakes, called dosas, are very popular. Yummy!

BARKO'S BLOG-TASTIC INDIA FACTS

Indian sweets are made from milk, coconut, nuts, sugar, and cream cheese. People make them at home or buy them from shops. You give boxes of sweets as gifts on special occasions, such as weddings and festivals.

Fun and games

Posted by: Ben Blog | 11 December at 3.32 p.m.

Next, we flew east to the city of Kolkata to watch a cricket match. Indians are crazy about cricket and play in the street, on the beach, or in the park – wherever they can find space. Members of the Indian cricket team are national heroes. When they are playing, the city comes to a stop.

BARKO'S BLOG-TASTIC INDIA FACTS

Every day, millions of Indians go to the movies to see the latest films. The films are blockbusters, packed with songs, dancing, and action. They are usually at least three hours long. I hope that this one is not sold out!

From TVs to tea leaves

Posted by: Ben Blog | 28 December at 8.23 a.m.

My laptop wasn't working properly, and I needed to get it fixed. So, we headed to Bangalore, India's centre for IT (information technology). Thousands of people work with computers here. Factories in India also make TVs, washing machines, and cars. This has made some Indians very rich, but millions of people are still desperately poor.

BARKO'S BLOG-TASTIC INDIA FACTS

Fancy a cup of tea? India grows hundreds of thousands of tonnes of tea and sells it to other countries. Here, in Darjeeling, tea is grown on huge **plantations**. Workers pick the leaves by hand.

And finally ...

Our trip is nearly over, and we have saved the best for last. We are here in Agra to see the Taj Mahal. It is one of the world's most famous buildings, so I took loads of pictures. It was built in the 1600s by **Mughal emperor** Shah Jahan in memory of his dead wife. What a sight!

BARKO'S BLOG-TASTIC INDIA FACTS

This amazing **mangrove** swamp grows around the Bay of Bengal. It is called the Sundarbans, and it is home to the very rare Bengal tiger. What was that noise?

India fact file

Area: 3,288,000 square kilometres
(1,269,500 square miles)

Population: 1,220,800,000 (2013)

Capital city: New Delhi

Other main cities: Mumbai; Kolkata

Languages: Hindi and 21 other official languages

Main religions: **Hinduism**; Islam;
Christianity; Sikhism

Highest mountain: Kanchenjunga
(8,598 metres / 28,209 feet)

Longest river: Brahmaputra
(2,840 kilometres/1,764 miles)

Currency: Indian rupee

India quiz

Find out how much you know about India with our quick quiz.

1. What is a **sari**?
a) an Indian sweet
b) an Indian piece of clothing
c) an Indian musical instrument

2. What does *namaste* mean?
a) hello
b) good-bye
c) how are you?

3. Where do **Hindus** worship?
a) in a mosque
b) in a church
c) in a temple

4. Which is the most popular sport in India?
a) football
b) kite-flying
c) cricket

5. What is this?

Answers
1. b
2. a
3. c
4. c
5. Taj Mahal

Glossary

dialect a language spoken in a small area or by a small number of people

emperor a ruler

Hindu a person who follows the Hinduism religion

Hinduism an Indian religion, followed by Hindus

inquisitive being interested in learning about the world

mangrove a tree that grows along some tropical coasts

Marco Polo an explorer who lived from about 1254 to 1324; he travelled from Italy to China

monsoon a wind that brings heavy rain

Mughal people who ruled India from the 1500s to the 1800s

plantation a large farm where crops, such as tea and bananas, are grown

rickshaw a small vehicle for carrying passengers, often pulled by a man on a bicycle

sandstone a soft, reddish rock

sari a long piece of cloth that is wrapped around a woman's body

slum an overcrowded part of a city where poor people live

Find out more

Books

India. (Countries Around the World), Ali Brownlie Bojang (Raintree, 2012)

India (My Country), Jillian Powell (Franklin Watts, 2013)

We Visit India (Your Land and My Land), Khadija Ejaz (Mitchell Lane Publishers, 2014)

Websites

kids.nationalgeographic.com/kids/places
The National Geographic website has lots of information, photos, and maps of countries around the world.

www.worldatlas.com
Packed with information about various countries, this website includes flags, time zones, facts, maps, and timelines.

Index